Inuit Indians

Caryn Yacowitz

Heinemann Library
Chicago, Illinois

Photo research by Alan Gottlieb
Maps by John Fleck
Production by Que-Net Media
Printed and bound in the United States by Lake Book Manufacturing, Inc.

07 06 05 04 03
10 9 8 7 6 5 4 3 2 1

Library of Congress Cataloging-in-Publication Data
Yacowitz, Caryn.
  Inuit Indians / Caryn Yacowitz.
      v. cm. -- (Native Americans)
Includes bibliographical references and index.
Contents: Land of ice and snow -- The people -- Hunting on the sea and land -- Fish, birds, and berries -- Warm clothing -- Inuit houses -- Dog sleds and skidoos -- Small groups -- Medicine, religion, and spirits -- Inuit games and storytelling -- Explorers and traders arrive -- Big changes -- The Inuits today -- Challenges and the future.
  ISBN 1-4034-0863-7 (lib. bdg.) -- ISBN 1-4034-4171-5 (pbk.)
  1. Inuit--Juvenile literature. [1. Inuit. 2. Eskimos. 3. Indians of North America--Arctic regions.] I. Title. II. Native Americans (Heinemann Library (Firm))
  E99.E7Y33 2003
  971.9004'9712--dc21

                              2003007469

Acknowledgments
The author and publisher are grateful to the following for permission to reproduce copyright material:
pp. 4, 5, 10, 11, 14, 20, 28, 30 Bryan & Cherry Alexander; pp. 7, 8 General Research Division/Astor, Lenox and Tilden Foundations/New York Public Library; p. 9 Galen Rowell/Corbis; p. 12 National Archives of Canada/PA129886; p. 13 Arctic Studies Center/National Museum of Natural History/Smithsonian Institution; p. 15 R. J. S. Tickle/NGS Image Collection; p. 16 Paul A. Souders/Corbis; p. 17 Roger Tidman/Corbis; p. 18 Northwind Picture Archives; p. 19 Library of Congress/Neg.#USZ62-083592; p. 21 Photo by Barry McWayne/Courtesy Anchorage Museum/Department of Anthropology/Smithsonian Institution/#153,639; pp. 22, 25 Northwest Territories Archives/Prince of Wales Northern Heritage Centre, Yellowknife; p. 23 Burt Glinn/Magnum Photos ; p. 24 National Archives of Canada/C-040364; p. 26 Library of Congress/Neg.# LC-C2688-581; p. 27 Library of Congress/Neg.# USZ62-12778

Cover photograph by Galen Rowell/Corbis

Special thanks to Helen Iguptak for her help in the preparation of this book.

Every effort has been made to contact copyright holders of any material reproduced in this book. Any omissions will be rectified in subsequent printings if notice is given to the publisher.

Some words are shown in bold, **like this.** You can find out what they mean by looking in the glossary.

Contents

Land of Ice and Snow

The Arctic lands circle the northern part of the earth. In North America, the Arctic stretches from present-day Alaska across Canada to the Atlantic Ocean. Greenland is also in the Arctic. Much of this area is covered with ice and snow all year long. On the **tundra,** the snow melts during the short summer. For a few weeks, grasses and bushes grow there.

The weather in the Arctic can be very cold. In the winter temperatures fall to negative 60 degrees Fahrenheit (negative 50 degrees Celsius). Summers can get very warm. For a few weeks during the winter, the Arctic is dark all day and all night. In the summer, it is light during the day and at night.

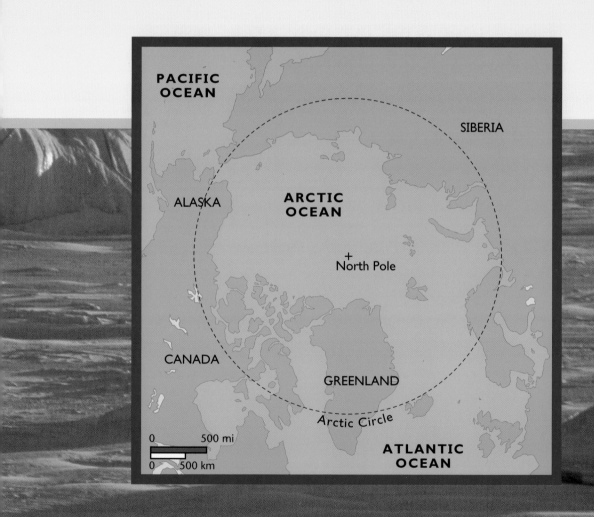

The People

The name *Inuit* means "the people." The first Inuit probably came to the Arctic areas of North America about 4,000 years ago. They came from present-day Siberia, in Russia. Some Inuit people still live in Siberia. Others traveled as far as present-day Greenland. The Inuit also live in present-day Alaska and Canada.

Inuit Words

In the Inuit language, the word *Inuk* is used to talk about one person. *Inuuk* means two people. *Inuit* is used to talk about three or more people.

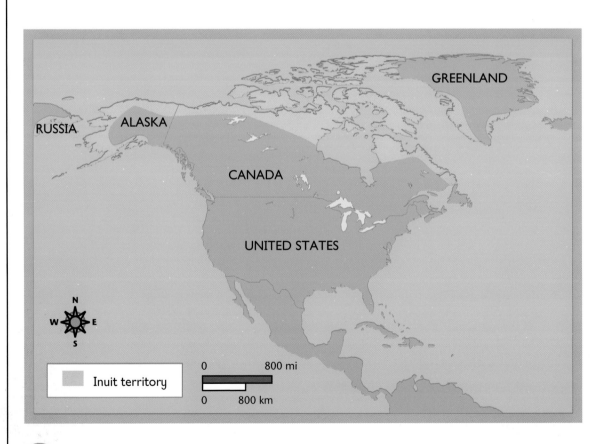

GREENLAND

RUSSIA   ALASKA

CANADA

UNITED STATES

N
W   E
S

Inuit territory

0   800 mi
0   800 km

This drawing from the 1820s shows a group of Inuit hunters.

The Inuit live in the coldest part of the world. Inuit people living in different areas of the Arctic sometimes have different **customs.** But all of them must deal with the cold. Their houses, food, clothing, and **traditions** are **adapted** to life in the Arctic.

Eskimo and Inuit

Until recently, the Inuit were known as Eskimos by the rest of the world. *Eskimo* is an Indian word that means "eats raw meat." The Inuit sometimes eat certain foods without cooking them.

Hunting on the Sea and Land

For thousands of years, the Inuit people hunted for most of their food. They built kayaks and *umiaqs* to hunt for seals, walruses, and whales. Kayaks are boats made of whalebone frames with sealskin stretched over them. A kayak holds one or two people. *Umiaqs* are larger boats that can hold about twelve hunters. Men hunted **sea mammals** with **harpoons** and **spears**.

This 1820s drawing shows Inuit hunters waiting by seal breathing holes. When a seal came up for air, a hunter would catch it.

8

Caribou move from place to place depending on the season.
*This caribou is on the **tundra**.*

On land, the Inuit hunted polar bears and **caribou** with bows and arrows. The Inuit depended on the caribou for food, clothing, and tools. They used all parts of the caribou including the **hide,** bones, and **antlers.** Nothing was wasted.

Hunting Together

Hunting whales and walruses was very dangerous. Groups of hunters worked together. The leader of the hunting group was a man whom the others trusted completely. Everyone shared the meat from the hunt. The meat was divided among the families.

Fish, Birds, and Berries

Most of the Inuit people's food comes from **caribou, sea mammals,** and polar bears. They also eat fish. The Inuit sometimes eat **salmon** and other fish raw. Some of the fish is dried so it can be eaten in the winter. It is hard to hunt and fish in winter. Sometimes the Inuit used to put fish and meat in holes cut into the ice. These ice cellars kept the meat from rotting.

The Inuit have many ways of keeping fish from rotting. Here an Inuk hunter is drying fish on a wood rack.

This Inuk man is using a net with a long handle to catch birds.

The Inuit used to be afraid of going hungry in the winter. They had to get as much food as possible during the short summer. The Inuit still catch small birds in nets. The birds are smoked over a fire to keep the meat from rotting. During the summer, the Inuit gather plants for food and medicine. They also gather berries on the **tundra.**

Today's Food
The Inuit still hunt and eat seals, polar bears, and whales. The meat gives them all the vitamins they need. They also buy some food in stores.

Warm Clothing

If the Inuit could not stay warm, they would quickly die from the cold. They invented many clever ways to keep themselves warm. They wore two **layers** of clothing. The bottom layer was made of animal skins with the fur worn against the body. The top layer was worn with the fur on the outside. The air between the two layers of clothing helped a person stay warm.

This Inuk man's sun goggles have narrow slits to see through

This parka is made from the intestines of a walrus.
The decorations are feathers.

The Inuit wore fur jackets called parkas or anoraks.
They wore long pants made of seal or polar bear
skins. The Inuit made waterproof boots from polar
bear **hides** or other skins. They sewed together the
intestines of walruses and other **sea mammals** to
make light, waterproof raincoats. The Inuit made
snowshoes from sealskin.

Inuit Houses

In the Inuit language, the word *iglu* means "snow house." The Inuit make *iglus* with large blocks of snow. They use about 35 blocks of snow to build a **domed** house. They fit the snow blocks together so it will be warm inside. Sometimes the Inuit use a block of ice to make a window. The long, low entrance helps keep the warm air inside.

Inuit Lamps

The Inuit made stone lamps to light their houses. They used seal oil in the lamps.

This iglu *does not have a long entrance. It has a block of snow that serves as a door.*

Qarmaqs were used all year long. This picture was taken during the warmer months. The dogs on the ground are taking a nap.

The Inuit used to build **sod** houses, or *qarmaqs*. These were more common than snow *iglus*. They used sod, rocks, whale bones, and wood— whatever they could find. Families built different houses for different times of the year. In the summer some Inuit people lived in tents made of sealskin. People moved from house to house following the animals they hunted for food.

Dog Sleds and Skidoos

Inuit people often use dog sleds to travel over ice and snow. The dogs can run long distances. They work together as a team. Their thick fur is **adapted** to the cold weather. Even in the coldest temperatures, sled dogs can sleep outside. Sometimes the Inuit use sled dogs to find seal breathing holes. Sled dogs are trained to quietly wait for a piece of seal meat.

The Inuit use between six and eight dogs to pull a sled.

There are no highways into many Inuit towns. The easiest way to get around is by skidoo.

Today the Inuit also use snowmobiles to travel. They call them *skidoos*. The Inuit often pull a sled behind the *skidoo. Skidoos* travel very fast over the snow and ice. But a *skidoo* is not as quiet as sled dogs. This makes it difficult to hunt when traveling with a *skidoo. Skidoos* also need expensive gasoline to run.

Howling Dogs

Sled dogs do not bark. They howl like wolves.

17

Small Groups

The Inuit lived in small groups. This meant there were not too many people to feed. They did not have chiefs. Instead, the best hunter in the group was often the leader. By working together and sharing, the group could live through the tough winters.

Inuit Children

Adults teach Inuit children to watch, listen, and be patient. They are also taught to help the community and honor the **elders.**

This painting shows a small Inuit village of iglus. It was painted in 1871.

18

An Inuk mother often carried her baby in a pouch on her back.

When a man and a woman got married, they lived near the man's relatives. It was important for the man to live near his own family. He would hunt with men from his family. The men needed to trust one another completely. Hunting was very dangerous.

Medicine, Religion, and Spirits

The Inuit believe that all things are connected to one another. This includes people, animals, and things that are not alive, like stones and wind. The Inuit call the **spirit** that is in everything *inua*.

*This carving by artist Yvonne Kayotak shows how Sedna created the **sea mammals**. The carving is made from a reindeer **antler**.*

This is a polar bear mask. It was used by the Inuit during ceremonies.

In some parts of the Arctic, Inuit men and women wore animal masks during dancing **ceremonies**. They **carved** bear and raven masks from wood and bone. **Medicine men** or **shamans** led winter **festivals**. One Inuit ceremony is the Bladder Dance. During this dance, the Inuit set free the spirits of all the animals killed during the year. This is one of the ways that the Inuit show respect for nature.

Inuit Games and Storytelling

The Inuit play games in the winter. In the string game, players make different shapes from string while singing songs. *Ajagaq* is another game. A large bone is tossed into the air and caught on a pointed bone. The Inuit also enjoy wrestling.

This Inuit game is a two-person tug-of-war. The goal is to pull the other person across a line.

*This Inuk **elder** is using a string figure to tell a story to children.*

Storytelling is also a winter activity. The Inuit people tell stories to remember their history, for entertainment, and to settle arguments. They also tell stories to tease one another and have fun. While telling stories, they play drums. In some places, fathers make story knives for their daughters. When a girl tells stories to her friends, she uses the knife to draw pictures in the ground or snow.

Explorers and Traders Arrive

The Inuit lived in the Arctic for thousands of years before they met people from other parts of the world. People in Europe and Asia did not imagine human beings could live in the cold Arctic. About four hundred years ago, an English explorer named Martin Frobisher was searching for a way to sail from the Atlantic Ocean to the Pacific Ocean. During the search, he met the Inuit of Canada.

This 1819 painting shows Inuit people paddling their kayaks out to meet Canadian traders.

The Inuit traded furs for all kinds of things. This Inuk man is trading white fox furs.

Traders came to the Arctic from Europe, America, and Russia. The Inuit way of life began to change. The Inuit began to trade furs and skins for guns, knives, and other things they wanted. Soon hunters who were not Inuit began to kill thousands of the **sea mammals.** Traders also brought **diseases** that killed many thousands of Inuit people. Sometimes, all of the people in a village died.

Big Changes

In 1867 the United States bought land from Russia. This land became the state of Alaska. Soon Americans were coming to Alaska to mine gold, catch whales, and hunt animals for their fur. The Inuit were no longer alone on their land. Some Alaskan Inuit began to live in towns. They no longer followed the **caribou** or the **sea mammals**.

*Inuit towns began to change after contact with traders and **settlers**. This photograph was taken in the early 1900s.*

*Commercial fishing brought jobs to Alaska. But it also made it harder for the Inuit to fish using **traditional** ways.*

In the 1900s, **commercial** fishing and oil drilling began in Alaska. This brought more changes. Often, Inuit families could not find enough fish or animals for food. Their land and water was not as clean. Also, the United States government did not let the Inuit fish and hunt as before. The government wanted to **protect** the animals. But many Inuit people starved. In 1980 the government passed a law that let the Inuit hunt again.

The Inuit Today

Today most Inuit people live in towns, in wood houses. They have to travel farther to hunt. Many older people speak the Inuit language, *Inuktitut*. Others speak *Inuktitut* at home and at Inuit government meetings.

Inuit Art

Inuit artists are famous for their stone **carvings.** They carve seals, polar bears, birds, and other animals.

These children are learning the Inuit language at a school in Nunavut.

28

In 1999 an Inuit territory was created in northern Canada. It is called Nunavut, which means "our land." Nunavut is controlled by the Inuit people. They believe that having control of their land again will help them solve problems and keep their **traditions.** Good jobs, health care, and good hunting grounds are important to the Inuit.

Challenges and the Future

The Inuit still believe in helping each other and sharing. They are connected to the sea, the land, and the animals. Young people learn about nature from **elders.** Many Inuit families live by hunting and fishing for their food. They may also make **carvings** to sell. Other Inuit people have jobs that pay them money. The Inuit hope to create more jobs by inviting **tourists** to their lands. They hope that each year more people will come to learn about their way of life.

*By gathering as a family, the Inuit keep their **traditions** alive.*

30

Glossary

adapt   change to fit new conditions

antler   horn of an animal of the deer family

caribou   large kind of deer with antlers

carve   cut into a shape with a knife or sharp tool

ceremony   event that celebrates a special occasion

commercial   having to do with making money

custom   something that has been done for a long time

disease   sickness

domed   with a round roof that is shaped like the top half of a globe

elder   older person

festival   day or time of celebration

harpoon   spear attached to a rope that is used to hunt whales and other sea animals

hide   skin of a large, dead animal, usually with the fur still on it

intestine   lower part of an animal's digestive system

layer   piece of something laid over another piece

medicine man   person with spiritual power

protect   keep from harm or danger

salmon   large fish that returns to the same river where it was born

sea mammal   warm-blooded animal that lives in the sea

settler   person who makes a home in a new place

shaman   religious leader or healer

sod   upper layer of soil that is bound into a thick mat by the roots of grass and other plants

spear   long, straight weapon with a sharp blade at one end

spirit   invisible force or being with special power

tourist   person who travels for pleasure

tradition   custom or story that has been passed from older people to younger people for a long time

tundra   flat plain without trees in cold arctic regions

More Books to Read

Alexander, Bryan, and Cherry Alexander. *What Do We Know about the Inuit?* Columbus, Ohio: Peter Bedrick Books, 2002.

Gray-Kanatiiosh, Barbara A. *Inuit.* Edina, Minn.: Checkerboard Library, 2002.

Santella, Andrew. *The Inuit.* Danbury, Conn.: Children's Press, 2001.

Steltzer, Ulli. *Building an Igloo.* New York: Henry Holt & Company, 1999.

Index